The Glory Within You

DR. STUART PATTICO

Sunesis Ministries

The Glory Within You

Copyright © 2014 Dr. Stuart Pattico

The right of Stuart Pattico to be identified as author of this work has been asserted by him in accordance with the Copyright, Designs, and Patents Act 1988.

All rights reserved.

No part of this publication may be reproduced or transmitted in any form or by any means, electronic or mechanical, including photocopy, recording, or any information storage and retrieval system, without permission in writing from the author.

ISBN 978-0-9928495-5-9

Unless otherwise indicated, Biblical quotations are from the Holy Bible, New King James Version Copyright © 1982 Thomas Nelson, Inc. Used by permission. All rights reserved.

Scripture quotations marked (CEV) are from the Contemporary English Version Copyright © 1991, 1992, 1995 by American Bible Society. Used by Permission.

Quotations marked KJV are from the Holy Bible, King James Version.

Quotations marked NEB are from The New English Bible: The New Testament © 'The Delegates of the Oxford University Press and the Syndics of the Cambridge University Press 1961, 1970.

Quotations marked NET are from the NET Bible® copyright ©1996-2006 by Biblical Studies Press, L.L.C. http://netbible.com All rights reserved.

Quotations marked NIV are taken from the HOLY BIBLE, NEW INTERNATIONAL VERSION. Copyright © 1973, 1978, 1984 by International Bible Society. Used by permission of Hodder and Stoughton Ltd, a member of the Hodder Headline Plc Group. All rights reserved. "NIV" is a registered trademark of International Bible Society. UK trademark number 1448790.

Wherever a part of a quotation is **bold** or underlined, this emphasis has been added by the author, and is not bold or underlined in the original quotation. Also, when any part of a quotation is in [square brackets], this has been added by the author for clarification, and is not part of the original quotation.

SUNESIS MINISTRIES

For more information, please visit:

WWW.STUARTPATTICO.COM

About the Author

DR. STUART PATTICO is an ordained full-time minister of the gospel. He has an itinerant preaching, teaching, and healing ministry to various churches, and has ministered in the UK and overseas.

Dr. Pattico is the author of several books. His earned qualifications include a Doctor of Ministry from Christian Leadership University, a Master of Arts in Bible & Ministry from King's College London, and a Bachelor of Science (Hons) in Computing & Information Systems from the University of London.

Dr. Pattico has also been a visiting lecturer for the Theology and Ministry Master's degree programme at King's College London.

He is happily married to Minister Andrea, who is an anointed speaker and worship leader. For more information and resources, please visit **WWW.STUARTPATTICO.COM**

Contents

Introduction	7
Chapter 1 – Like Father, Like Son	9
Chapter 2 – A New Creation	19
Chapter 3 – The Spiritual Man	23
Chapter 4 – A Dwelling Place for God's Glory	31
Chapter 5 – Living in the Glory	39
Conclusion	51
Appendix	53

Introduction

The book you are holding in your hands is all about the glory that God has put within you.

Whether you realise it or not, in Christ, you are an awesome sight to behold. This is because God's glory is inside you. Yet, many Christians do not realise how glorious they are. They view themselves as insignificant in the grand scheme of things. However, it is impossible to be insignificant when the glory of God is inside you. The Hebrew word translated "glory" literally means "weight". In biblical times, a person who had a high social standing and great wealth was automatically an esteemed, or we could say "weighty", person in the society. The fact that God's glory is in you makes you a significant, or "weighty" person.

The glory of God is also associated with "light" (see Isaiah 60:1). God's glory is the shining forth of His presence. Therefore, when the glory of God was said to "appear" to people, it meant that there was a special shining forth of God's presence. When we begin to see how glorious we are in Christ, the amazing thing is that others will see the glory in us too. Our glory, which God has given us, will shine forth.

As you read this short book, it is my prayer that you will see the great glory that God has put inside of you, and that this glory will shine forth and impact the world around you.

Shalom,

Dr. Stuart Pattico

Chapter 1 - Like Father, Like Son

God has put His very own glory inside of us. As we will see in this book, this glory is to be discovered within the context of our new nature in Christ Jesus. If we wish to radiate the glory that is within us, it is therefore essential that we understand our identity in Christ. However, we can only know who we are by knowing who Jesus is. We can only know our identity by knowing the identity of Christ, for the Word of God tells us that "...**as He [Jesus] is, so are we in this world**" (1 John 4:17).

So, who then is Jesus? Well, in the following passage, John the apostle tells us something very important about Him:

> In the beginning was the Word, and the Word was with God, and the Word was God... And the Word became flesh and dwelt among us...
> (John 1:1, 14)

In this passage, Jesus is called "the Word". We know that "the Word" is Jesus because in verse 14 it says, "**the Word became flesh** and dwelt among us". This passage informs us that Jesus was already there when all things began, and that He was with God. Furthermore, we are told, "the Word was God".

When John said, "the Word was God", the original Greek does not have a definite article before the word "God". In Greek grammar, a definite article is like our English word "the". It is similar to the gesture of someone pointing at something and saying "this one". When there is no definite article, it sometimes indicates that the word following is characteristic of the subject of that clause. For example, in 1 John 1:5 we read, "God is light". The original Greek has no definite article before "light", which indicates that "light" is characteristic of "God". That is, the nature of God is light.   Even so, the absence of the definite article before "God" in the last clause of John 1:1 indicates that "God" is characteristic of "the Word" (who is the subject of that clause). John is ascribing the fullness of God's essence to the Word. He is basically saying that **the Word is everything that God is**. In light of the construction in the original Greek, the best translation of John 1:1 I have come across is found in the New English Bible. It reads as follows:

> When all things began, the Word already was. The Word dwelt with God, and **what God was, the Word was**.
> (John 1:1 NEB)

So, in this verse, John is saying that Jesus has always been there. He has always been with the Father, and **He is just like the Father**. Because Jesus is just like the Father, He reveals the Father perfectly. For this reason, John calls Jesus "the Word". A "word" is a way by which we communicate ourselves to others. Even so, Jesus is the perfect communication of God. He reveals and communicates the Father perfectly because He is just like Him. We could say, "Like Father, like Son"!

This is why Jesus is called "the Son of God". In order to fully understand what this means, it is useful to be aware of two key Greek words translated "son" in the Bible. These two Greek words are *teknon* and *huios*. *Teknon* indicates that one is a son by virtue of the fact that they have been given birth to. *Huios* indicates that one is a son by virtue of the relationship with the parent, or because they exhibit the characteristics of the parent. For example, Jesus called James and John "Sons [huios] of Thunder" in Mark 3:17. The Greek word for "sons" he used there was *huios*. They were called such because they exhibited the characteristics of thunder. So, *teknon* speaks of a biological son. But *huios* speaks of a son by relationship or similarity.

Now, here is what is important to realise: in the Greek, Jesus is never called the *teknon* of God. In the expression "the Son of God", the Greek word used is always *huios*. There was never a moment in eternity when God gave birth to Jesus. Jesus is not God's *teknon*. Jesus has always existed. The Father and the Son have always existed together throughout eternity. They have always had a Father-Son relationship, and the Son has always been exactly like the Father. This is why the Bible calls Jesus the *Huios* of God. He is God's Son by relationship and similarity. Jesus is just like the Father: "Like Father, like Son".

Because Jesus is everything that the Father is, Jesus is therefore the perfect revelation of the Father. That's why He said:

> He who has seen Me has seen the Father
> (John 14:9)

To see Jesus is to see the Father, because the Son is just like the Father. We see this same truth also in Hebrews 1:3:

> [3] The Son is the radiance of his [the Father's] glory and the representation of his essence
> (Hebrews 1:3, NET)

Jesus is the radiance of God's brilliance and is the perfect representation of His very essence. As such, if you want to know what God is like, all you need to do is to look at Jesus! Whatever your image of God is, make sure that it is consistent with the person of Jesus Christ. He reveals the Father perfectly.

When Jesus was on earth, He went around revealing the Father to people. He said to Philip:

> [7] "If you had known Me, you would have known My Father also; and from now on you know Him and have seen Him."
> (John 14:7)

No one can come to know and understand God without seeing the Son. He is the revelation of the Father. As John said at the beginning of his Gospel:

> No one has ever seen God. The only Son, who is truly God and is closest to the Father, has shown us what God is like.
> (John 1:18 CEV)

No one has seen the Father at any time. But His Son, Jesus Christ, has revealed Him to us.

Now, what does all this have to do with us? What does this have to do with the glory that is within us?

Well, let's go back to what John said in 1 John 4:17:

> ...as He [Jesus] is, so are we in this world
> (1 John 4:17)

We are "as He is". That is, we are just like Jesus! Let the magnitude of that statement sink in for a few moments….
Even as Jesus went around revealing the Father to people, the calling on our lives is to show people the Father. As He is, so are we in this world!

It is one thing to understand that Jesus is the Son of God. But it is another thing to realise that we are sons and daughters of God, and have partaken of Christ's Sonship. Let us consider what Paul wrote in the following verse:

> [6] And because you are sons, God has sent forth **the Spirit of His Son** into your hearts, crying out, "Abba, Father!"
> (Galatians 4:6)

Paul states that God has sent "the Spirit of His Son" into our hearts. This is something that happened to every believer the moment they became born again - The Spirit is given "because you are sons". Notice also that Paul refers to "the Spirit of His Son". He could have used the phrase "the Holy Spirit", as the Spirit of Jesus is the Holy Spirit. However, Paul intentionally refers to the Spirit as "the Spirit of His Son". He does this to emphasise that we have received the Spirit of Jesus and are therefore able to call God "Abba, Father!" just as Jesus calls Him "Abba, Father!" We have partaken of His Sonship! For this reason, Paul refers to Jesus as "the firstborn among many brethren" (Romans 8:29). Jesus is the elder brother; we are His younger brothers and sisters. We are part of the same family, and the presence of His Spirit in our hearts enables us to enter into the relationship that He Himself has with the Father. Indeed, as Paul states, the Spirit of Jesus within us is crying out, "Abba, Father!" (Galatians 4:6).

Notice that it is the Holy Spirit within us that enables us to personally experience the relationship that the Son has with the Father. Paul also wrote the following about the Spirit's role in relation to our position as sons:

> [14] For as many as are led by the Spirit of God, these are sons of God.
> (Romans 8:14)

Paul here states that those who are led by the Spirit are "sons" of God. The Greek word he uses for "sons" is *huios*. As we have seen, this Greek word speaks of a son by virtue of his relationship with, or his similarity to, the parent. Paul is saying that by being led by the Holy Spirit, we can enjoy an intimate relationship of sonship with the Father, and also behave in a manner that shows others what the Father is like. The principle of "like Father, like son" does not only apply to the Father and Jesus, it also applies to the Father and all those who are led by the Spirit! Those who are led by the Spirit are just like the Father and show people what He is like. In the following passage, Paul describes how those who are led by the Spirit will behave:

> [22] But the fruit of the Spirit is love, joy, peace, longsuffering, kindness, goodness, faithfulness,

> [23] gentleness, self-control. Against such there is no law.
> (Galatians 5:22-23)

When someone is led by the Holy Spirit they will behave in that manner. As we live in that way, we show by our conduct what our heavenly Father is like. Jesus also taught us the principle of behaving like our Father when He said the following:

> [44] But I say to you, love your enemies, bless those who curse you, do good to those who hate you, and pray for those who spitefully use you and persecute you, [45] **that you may be sons of your Father** in heaven; for He makes His sun rise on the evil and on the good, and sends rain on the just and on the unjust.
> (Matthew 5:44-45)

No matter if people are good or evil, God still causes the sun to rise upon them and still sends them rain. Jesus teaches that we are to emulate the Father's kindness, even to those who hate us, because that is what the Father does. When we do so, Jesus says that we will be "sons of your Father in heaven". The word He uses for "sons" here is *huios*. As we have seen, this word speaks of a son by virtue of his similarity to the parent. From the moment we are born again, we become a child of God. But we only become a mature son or daughter when we begin to emulate our Father's characteristics. That is why Jesus uses the word *huios* in this verse. He is saying that when we love our enemies, we are emulating our heavenly Father, and are therefore sons and daughters whose behaviour resembles the Father.

Before He ascended to heaven, Jesus said the following to His disciples:

> As the Father has sent Me, I also send you.
> (John 20:21)

Jesus said to His disciples that in the same way the Father had sent Him, He was now sending them. In other words, they were being commissioned with the same task that the Father gave to the Son. Even as the Son went about showing the Father to people, now the disciples were to do the same! The same calling is on our lives too. We are now to show the Father's love, presence, and heart to others, even as Jesus did. We are called to be carriers of the Father's presence and glory so that people may see the Father by looking at us!

Being aware of this truth should radically transform our self-image. I can assure you that Jesus didn't suffer from low self-esteem. After all, He is the radiance of the Father's glory! However, that same glory is in you. You have partaken of His Sonship. There is great glory in you! So shake off any inferiority complex and low self-esteem you may have. Realise that by virtue of the fact that you are a son or daughter of God, having partaken of the Sonship of Jesus, you are now clothed with the Father's glory. You are just like Him, having limitless strength and potential in your inner-being. You have been "born-again" and are a wonderful new creation in Christ Jesus. Old things have passed away; behold, all things have become new! (2 Corinthians 5:17)

Reflective Questions:

How does knowing that you have partaken of Christ's Sonship affect your self-image?

How does knowing that you have partaken of Christ's Sonship affect your sense of purpose in this world?

Chapter 2 - A New Creation

At the beginning of the last chapter, I mentioned that the glory that God has placed within us is to be discovered within the context of our new nature in Christ Jesus. In the sections that follow, we will dig into this thought, and consider precisely what our new nature in Christ is.

We will begin by considering what it means to be "saved". Often when we think of being "saved", one of the first things that comes to mind is that we have escaped hell. However, when the Bible refers to our salvation, it is referring to something that goes far beyond escaping hell. In fact, escaping hell is merely the by-product of our salvation. To help us appreciate this, let us examine what Paul the apostle wrote in Titus 3:5:

> not by works of righteousness which we have done, but according to His mercy He saved us, through the washing of regeneration and renewing of the Holy Spirit
> (Titus 3:5)

In this verse, Paul reveals that our salvation is the result of two things. He states that our salvation has occurred "through the washing of **regeneration**" and "**renewing** of the Holy Spirit". Let us first consider the word "regeneration". If I "generate" power, I am "producing" power. To "generate" means to "produce". Now that you are "saved" you have been "reproduced". You are not who you used to be. This is not simply because you have made a decision to be good and to behave differently. No, you have quite literally been regenerated. In other words, you are a brand new product.

Paul then goes on to refer to salvation as resulting from "renewing of the Holy Spirit". This simply means that the Holy Spirit has made you "new". For Paul, a saved person is one who has been made new, and this is what he alludes to in the following verse:

> [17] Therefore, if anyone *is* in Christ, *he is* a new creation; old things have passed away; behold, all things have become new.
> (2 Corinthians 5:17)

Notice that Paul refers to "anyone" who is in Christ. The word "anyone" includes everyone and excludes no one. Therefore, if you are in Christ, then he's referring to you. Paul states that in Christ, you are a "new creation". Now, this "new creation" is not something that you will one day become. Paul does not say "if anyone fasts and prays enough, he is a new creation". He doesn't say, "if anyone goes to Bible school, he is a new creation". As good as fasting, prayer, and Bible study are; they are not what make you a new creation. Paul simply states, "if anyone *is* in Christ, he **is** a new creation". You are a new creation right now, simply because you have put your faith in Jesus Christ. That's why Paul wrote the following:

> For by grace you have been **saved through faith**...
> (Ephesians 2:8)

We have been saved through "faith". If your faith is in Jesus Christ, then you have been "saved". You have been regenerated and renewed. You are a new creation in Christ. Whether you realise it or not, when Jesus died on the cross, the old you died with Him. As Paul elsewhere states: "our old man was crucified with *Him*" (Romans 6:6). And when Jesus rose up from the grave, we rose up with Him as a brand new creation. Peter alludes to this when he says:

> [God] has **begotten us again** to a living hope **through the resurrection** of Jesus Christ from the dead
> (1 Peter 1:3)

Have you ever wondered why Jesus' body was resurrected? After all, He could have just gone back to heaven as a spirit, couldn't He? Well, He was resurrected so that we could rise with Him as a brand new creation. This is what it means to be "born again". Notice that Peter refers to the fact that God has "begotten us again", and states that this has been accomplished "through the resurrection of Jesus Christ from the dead". Jesus was resurrected so that we could be "born again" as brand new creatures.

Reflective Questions:

How does knowing that you are a new creation now alter the way you view yourself?

Did you previously think of yourself as having already become a new creation, or did you think that it was something you were trying to achieve?

Chapter 3 – The Spiritual Man

In the last chapter, we saw that we have become a "new creation" through the resurrection of Jesus Christ. But what exactly is this new creation? In John 3:6, Jesus said the following about the new birth:

> That which is born of the flesh is flesh, and that which is born of the Spirit is spirit.
> (John 3:6)

In this verse, Jesus describes being "born again" as being born "of the Spirit". To be "born again" is to be born of the Holy Spirit. Jesus further informs us that the part of us that is born again is our spirit – "that which is born of the Spirit **is spirit**". Each of us consists of three parts – spirit, soul and body. Paul made this clear when he wrote, "may your whole spirit, soul, and body be preserved blameless" (1 Thessalonians 5:23). Our body is the outer, physical part of us. The Greek word translated "soul" is *psuche* from which we get the English word "psyche". Our soul is our mind (intellect), will, and emotions[1]. The soul continues to exist through the spirit when the body dies (Revelation 6:9-10). Our spirit is our spiritual nature. It is our innermost being. Peter calls the human spirit the "hidden man of the heart":

> But let it be **the hidden man of the heart**, in that which is not corruptible, even the ornament of a meek and quiet **spirit**...
> (1 Peter 3:4 KJV)

---

[1] In the Bible, the word "soul" is also sometimes used simply as a reference to a person.

Now, when you became "born again", it was not your body that was born again. I am quite sure that you have the same body that you had before you were saved! Our bodies will not be saved until Jesus comes again and we receive new bodies just like His body:

> [20] For our citizenship is in heaven, from which we also eagerly wait for the Savior, the Lord Jesus Christ, [21] who will transform our lowly body that it may be conformed to His glorious body...
> (Philippians 3:20-21)

It was not your soul (i.e. mind, will, and emotions) that was born again either. No, your soul is in a *process* of being saved. Consider what James wrote in his letter to believers:

> ...receive with meekness the implanted word, which is **able to save your souls**.
> (James 1:21)

James wrote that to believers. Notice that he said that the word of God was "able" to save their souls. Apparently, those believers' souls weren't saved yet! It is important to realise that the salvation of our soul is an on-going process, which occurs as we yield to God's word. Remember, to be "saved" is much more than escaping hell. To be saved is to be transformed. Our souls are still in a process of transformation. That's why you may still struggle with your emotions from time to time. Your emotions have not yet been "born again". Neither has our mind. That's why Paul told the Romans to "be transformed by the renewing of your mind" (Romans 12:2). As our mind is renewed, our soul begins to experience a transformation. In the original Greek, "transformed" is in the present tense, which indicates that an ongoing process is in view. As our minds are renewed, and we begin to think the way that God wants us to, our soul experiences a transformation and we come into alignment with who God has called us to be.

So, it was not your body or soul that was "born again". The part of you that has been born again is your spirit. God has given you a brand new spirit. Your new spirit is the "new you". The key to living victoriously as a Christian is to live as a spirit; after all, Jesus told us that "God *is* Spirit, and those who worship Him must worship **in spirit** and truth" (John 4:24). The key for the Christian is to live as a spirit.

To illustrate the importance of living as a spirit, let us consider the following scenario. Let's imagine that someone were to hit you. How would you want to respond? Well, your flesh would probably want to hit the person back! Your soul would likely feel angry and infuriated that this person has done this to you. But your spirit would want to turn the other cheek. That's what Jesus told us to do (Matthew 5:39). Now, to turn the other cheek does not mean that we say to the person, "Hey, here's my other cheek, please hit me on that one also!" No, that would just be stupid. What it means is that when someone does us bad, we turn around and do them good. The other cheek is the cheek of righteousness.

Notice that I said that your spirit would *want* to turn the other cheek. It doesn't just begrudgingly feel that it *has to* because it's the religious thing to do. No, your spirit is now a new creation and its only desire is to do what is pleasing in God's sight. Your spirit has been "born again" and thinks differently to your flesh. This is because your flesh still has the sinful nature (Romans 7:23), whereas your spirit has been made a new creation.

Let us illustrate this concept further. Have you ever not *felt* like worshipping God? There have probably been times when you have not felt like doing so. But what part of you feels that way? It is only your flesh and soul that will ever feel like that. Whilst your soul may not be in the mood, your spirit is always in the mood to worship. Your spirit always wants to worship God. Likewise, I'm sure there have been plenty of times when you have not felt like reading the Bible. Again, that's your flesh and soul. Your spirit on the other hand wants to read the Word. This is why Jesus said: "The spirit is willing, but the flesh is weak" (Matthew 26:41). Your spirit is always in the mood to do spiritual things; it's the flesh that is weak. So, next time you are not in the mood for spiritual things, just say to yourself: "that's just my flesh talking, my spirit wants to do this". When you live with that consciousness, you will live victoriously.

Let us move on now to consider something else that Jesus said:

> "Most assuredly, I say to you, unless one is **born again**, he cannot see the kingdom of God." (John 3:3)

Notice the phrase "born again". The word "again" translates the Greek word *anōthen* which literally means "from above". It comes from the Greek word *anō* which means "upward" or "on the top". Therefore, to be born again really means to be born "from above".

Now, it is your spirit that has been born again. This means that your spirit has been born "from above". Therefore, you didn't get your new spirit from your parents. You got your body from your parents; but your born again spirit didn't come from them – your spirit has been born "from above". Let us consider what John wrote:

> [12] But as many as received Him, to them He gave the right to become children of God, to those who believe in His name: [13] who were born, not of blood, nor of the will of the flesh, nor of the will of man, but of God.
> (John 1:13)

According to the above passage, those of us who have received Jesus, have not been born of blood or human beings; we have been born "of God". This is a reference to our new spirit. Our new spirit did not come from our parents; it came from God Himself. Our new spirit is not from this planet. Our spirit has come "from above". As far as our spiritual nature is concerned, we are aliens. We come from a different realm and a different dimension altogether. It is important that you begin to see yourself very differently; you are not ordinary. You are different, you are meant to stick out because you are born from another dimension.

Have you noticed that you have certain desires and dreams within you that seem impossible? That's because your spirit is not from this realm where things are limited. In the world of athletics, athletes are often trying to break records, whether it be their personal best, or the even the world record. They are trying to break through barriers, or "limitations". But you, that is the "real you", come from a realm where there are no limits. The dimension you come from is naturally supernatural.

Notice that I have referred to your spirit as the "real you". One of the reasons that Christians do not live victoriously is because they view themselves in the wrong way. They often view themselves as a body that has a soul and a spirit. Perhaps you have thought of yourself in that way – as primarily a physical being that has a spirit somewhere deep inside them. But you are not a body that has a soul and a spirit. **You are a spirit**, that *has* a soul, and *lives* in a body. We do not merely have a spirit, **we are a spirit**. If you view yourself as a body, then your flesh will have the upper hand. If you view yourself as a soul, then your intellect and emotions will have the dominance. But when you view yourself as a spirit, that has a soul, and lives in a body, then you will realize that your body and soul are subject to you, and that you are a spirit-being. You will therefore be able to live the victorious Christian life. As we have seen, Jesus said, "that which is born of the Spirit **is spirit**" (John 3:6). Not only does this indicate that it is your spirit that was born again, it also shows us the identity of the one who is born again – he or she "is spirit"! As a born again person, it is essential that you see yourself as a spirit-being that has a soul, and lives in a body. Your body does not call the shots. You are no longer led by your body and by what your flesh wants because you realize that you are a spirit. You are a spirit that has been regenerated and renewed.

On a particular occasion I was teaching these truths to a group. I asked them the following question: "how close do you feel to God?" One of those present responded by saying, "Depends". If we are honest, that is sometimes the case with us. How close we *feel* to God may depend on the circumstances and what is going on in our life. However, that feeling is not our spirit. Such a feeling comes from the soul and body. If we were to go by the reality of our spirit we would realize that we are constantly close to God. Let us consider what Paul wrote in the following passage:

> [16] Or do you not know that he who is joined to a harlot is one body *with her?* For "the two," He says, "shall become one flesh." [17] But he who is joined to the Lord is one spirit *with Him.*
> (1 Corinthians 6:16-17)

Paul states that if a man has sex with a harlot, he becomes "one body" with her due to the act of intercourse. Literally, the two become "one flesh" in that act. Even so, such is the closeness of our spiritual relationship with the Lord that Paul states that we have become "one spirit" with Him. In other words, your spirit and the Holy Spirit have been fused together; and that happened the moment you became born again. The Holy Spirit entered your heart and joined Himself to the real you, your spirit. Your soul may not feel that way, but your spirit does. Your spirit has been fused together with the Holy Spirit, so that you are now "one spirit". You and the Holy Spirit are tight. You cannot be separated, you are "one". That's how close you are to God. This means that God is never ever far from you. He quite literally never leaves you or forsakes you. Jesus said, "I am with you always till the end of the age" (Matthew 28:20), so if you ever feel that God is far from you, it's not true!

Reflective Questions:

How have your previously thought of yourself? As a body, that has a spirit and soul? As a soul, that has a body and spirit? Or as a spirit, that has a soul, and lives in a body?

How will viewing yourself as a spirit-being, that has a soul, and lives in a body impact the way you live?

Chapter 4 - A Dwelling Place for God's Glory

In the last chapter, we saw that our spirit has become one with the Lord. The fact that we are "one spirit" with the Lord also reminds us of our identity as God's dwelling place. Paul the apostle wrote to the Corinthians and told them, "you are the temple of the living God" (2 Corinthians 6:16). Corporately and individually, we are the temple of God. The fact that you are the temple of God indicates that the Temple and the tabernacle in the Old Testament (which were built to be a dwelling place of God) were symbolic of you. They were a prophetic shadow of what you are.

The tabernacle had three sections: "the court of the tabernacle", the "holy place", and the "holy of holies". The court corresponds to your body. It was the outermost section and contained the altar, which is where the sacrifices were offered. Paul said about our bodies, "present your bodies a living sacrifice" (Romans 12:1), which relates to the altar.

The "holy place" corresponds to your soul (i.e. the mind, will, and emotions). It was the first section within the tent. The "holy place" contained the lampstand, the shewbread and the altar of incense. The lampstand speaks of light or illumination, which relates to the mind. The shewbread speaks of strength, which relates to the will. The altar of incense relates to the emotions.

The "holy of holies" corresponds to your spirit. It was the innermost part of the tabernacle, much like your spirit is the innermost part of you. It was separated from the "holy place" by a veil. The "holy of holies" was the compartment of the tabernacle in which God dwelt. This is because His throne was there. His throne was the ark of the covenant, which was a chest that had a cover known as the mercy seat. The mercy seat was adorned with two heavenly beings known as cherubim. It was understood that God dwelt between the cherubim, as indicated by the following verses.

> ...the ark of the covenant of the LORD of hosts, **who dwells *between* the cherubim**...
> (1 Samuel 4:4)

> ...the ark of God the LORD, who dwells *between* the cherubim...
> (1 Chronicles 13:6)

> [15] Then Hezekiah prayed before the LORD, and said: "O LORD God of Israel, *the One* who dwells *between* the cherubim...
> (2 Kings 19:15)

As God dwelt between the cherubim, the location of the ark (i.e. the "holy of holies") is the place where God would meet Moses and speak to him from. God said to Moses:

> And there I will meet with you, and I will speak with you from above the mercy seat, from between the two cherubim which are on the ark of the Testimony, about everything which I will give you in commandment to the children of Israel.
> (Exodus 25:22)

Thus, whilst the entire tabernacle was built to be a dwelling place of God (Exodus 25:8), the "holy of holies" was the particular compartment of the tabernacle where God would appear and speak from.

Even so, your spirit is the part of you where God dwells and speaks from. According to Paul, the human heart is the dwelling place of the Holy Spirit:

> [6] And because you are sons, God has sent forth the Spirit of His Son **into your hearts**, crying out, "Abba, Father!" (Galatians 4:6)

Notice that the Spirit has been sent "into your hearts". As we have seen, your spirit is the "hidden man of the heart" (1 Peter 3:4 KJV). When the Holy Spirit entered your heart, He fused Himself together with your spirit, so that your spirit is now one with the Holy Spirit – "he who is joined to the Lord is one spirit *with Him*" (1 Corinthians 6:17). As God dwells in your spirit, it is from your spirit that God speaks.

On a particular occasion, the ark stayed in the house of a man called Obed-edom. The presence of the ark in his house caused his household and all he had to experience uncommon blessing (2 Samuel 6:11-12). The blessing was so great that it caused King David to have the ark removed from there to the city of David, and inside the tent that David had pitched for it (2 Samuel 6:12,17). Because the ark (i.e. the dwelling place of God) is now in our spirit, our spirit is wonderfully blessed. In fact, because our spirit is so blessed, it is impossible for our spirit to become any more blessed than it already is. Paul told the Ephesians that God "has blessed us with every spiritual blessing" (Ephesians 1:3). There are no more blessings for your spirit to receive, as you have already been blessed with "every spiritual blessing". Because many see themselves as primarily a physical or intellectual being, they live way below the level of blessing they have in Christ. It is only when you see yourself as a spirit-being, that has a soul and dwells in a body, that you can live at the level God has made available to us.

In the book of Leviticus, God said, "I will appear in the cloud above the mercy seat" (Leviticus 16:2). In the Bible, "the cloud" is associated with God's glory. For example, in Exodus we read that "the glory of the LORD appeared in the cloud" (Exodus 16:10). The cloud itself was not the glory of God; it would seem that the cloud shielded the people from the brightness of God's glory. Interestingly, the cherubim who overshadowed the mercy seat are called "the cherubim of glory" in Hebrews 9:5. Even so, it would seem that the ark was understood to represent the glory of God. When the ark was captured by the Philistines, it was said:

> "The glory has departed from Israel, for the ark of God has been captured."
> (1 Samuel 4:22)

This indicates that the ark was understood to be a prophetic symbol of the glory of God. Even so, just as God put His glory in the innermost section of the tabernacle – in the "holy of holies"; God has placed His glory in your innermost being - in your spirit. This glory is the Lord Jesus Himself. Indeed, Jesus is called in Scripture, "the Lord of glory" (1 Corinthians 2:8). He lives inside of you. You have become "one spirit" with the Lord of glory according to 1 Corinthians 6:17. Therefore, our spirit is now united with the glory of God. This indicates that our spirit has taken on a new glorious and supernatural nature – the nature of the Lord of glory Himself. To appreciate this, let us go back to the book of Genesis, when the first woman was created:

> [21] And the LORD God caused a deep sleep to fall on Adam, and he slept; and He took one of his ribs, and closed up the flesh in its place. [22] Then the rib which the LORD God had taken from man He made into a woman, and He brought her to the man. [23] And Adam said: "This *is* now **bone of my bones** And **flesh of my flesh**; She shall be called Woman, Because she was taken out of Man."
> (Genesis 2:21-23)

In those verses, we learn how the first woman was made (who later became known as Eve). A part of Adam constituted the physical material from which Eve was formed. Eve was made of the same "stuff" as the man. Therefore, Adam described her as "bone of my bones", and "flesh of my flesh". Keeping that in mind, let us now consider what Paul wrote about us:

> [30] For we are members of His [Christ's] body, **of His flesh and of His bones**.
> (Ephesians 5:30)

Notice that Paul says that we are members of Christ's flesh and bones. The phrase "of His flesh and of His bones" is adapted from the passage we just read in Genesis 2:21-23. Paul is intentionally drawing on the Genesis account of Eve's formation to inform us of our spiritual identity in Christ. Even as Eve was formed from Adam's body, we have been formed from Christ ("we are members of... His flesh and of His bones"). Even as Eve was made of the same "stuff" as Adam, our new spirit has been made from the same "stuff" as Jesus Christ! No wonder John states that "... as He is, so are we in this world" (1 John 4:17). Spiritually, we are made from the same glorious substance as Jesus Christ Himself!

Paul shows us this same truth again in the following passage:

> [10] and [you] have put on the new *man* who is renewed in knowledge according to the image of Him who created him, [11] where there is neither Greek nor Jew, circumcised nor uncircumcised, barbarian, Scythian, slave *nor* free, but Christ *is* all and in all.
> (Colossians 3:10-11)

Paul begins by stating that the believers have put on the "new man". The new man is our new spirit – the part of you that has become regenerated. He then goes on to tell us something very important about the new man. The "new man" is "neither Jew nor Greek". This simply means that the worldly classifications of race do not apply to your new spirit. Your spirit is not black, white, or Asian etc. This is evident from the fact that your new spirit is not from this world, it is "from above". Furthermore, Paul mentions that the new man is not "barbarian, Scythian, slave *nor* free". Barbarians did not speak Greek, and were thought to be uncivilised. Scythians (known for their brutality) were considered to be little better than wild beasts. Paul is telling us that the secular distinctions of class do not apply to our new spirit. So then, what is the race and class of our spirit? Paul tells us in the last clause: "but **Christ *is* all** and in all" (Colossians 3:11). Notice that he does not only say that Christ is in all. No, Paul begins by saying that "Christ *is* all". He takes the word "Christ" and uses it to define all believers. In other words, Paul is defining a new race and class called "Christ" of which we are all a part. The new man in Christ Jesus belongs to a brand new race and class called "Christ". You can therefore say, "My race is Christ".

Christ lives in us, but His presence in our hearts has also redefined us, insomuch that He has become our new race. He is our new race, He is our new class, we live for Him and He's the centre of our lives. Everything revolves around Him, and this new life that we have in Him is all about Him. The fact that our spirit is made from the same glorious substance as Jesus Christ Himself indicates that inherently, our spirit is full of His glory. Our spirit contains the life and nature of Christ Himself, and this means that His glory fills us. It is impossible for it to be any other way. Paul knew that this was the case, and so he prayed a special prayer for the Ephesians. Let us look closely at what he prayed, noting carefully the words in bold:

> [15] Therefore I also, after I heard of your faith in the Lord Jesus and your love for all the saints, [16] do not cease to give thanks for you, making mention of you in my prayers: [17] that the God of our Lord Jesus Christ, the Father of glory, may give to you **the spirit of wisdom and revelation** in the knowledge of Him, [18] the eyes of your understanding being enlightened; **that you may know** what is the hope of His calling, what are **the riches of the**

glory of His inheritance in the saints (Ephesians 1:15-18)

Paul tells the Ephesians about his prayer for them. He mentions that he prayed that God would give them the spirit of wisdom and revelation so that they would know certain things. One thing that Paul wanted them to know about was "the riches of the glory of His [God's] inheritance in the saints". Notice where the riches of the glory of God's inheritance are. Paul explicitly states that the riches of the glory are "in the saints". In other words, Paul wanted them to know the glory that God has placed within them! Are you aware of the glory that God has placed in you by virtue of your new identity in Christ? There is tremendous glory that you are carrying and your purpose in life is to go about the earth and release that glory wherever you go. That's why you are here. You are here to let your light shine. You are here to let this glory that is in you shine, that others may see your good works and glorify God (Matthew 5:16).

Reflective Questions:

To what extent do you walk with conscious awareness that you are a carrier of God's glory?

How does knowing that your spirit is made of the same glorious substance as Christ impact your sense of potential?

Chapter 5 - Living in the Glory

In the last chapter, we saw that the glory of God is in your spirit. Your spirit has been saturated with the glory of the Lord. Therefore, in order to live a life in the glory, all we need to do is to live from our spirit. When we do so, we live from the glory that is inside of us.

In the New Testament, we are exhorted, "Walk in the Spirit, and you will not fulfil the lust of the flesh". The simple key to living victoriously as a Christian is to walk in the Spirit, and not in the flesh. But how can we do this? How do we "walk in the Spirit"? The key is to understand that the Holy Spirit has become one with our spirit (1 Corinthians 6:17). As such, we can walk in the Holy Spirit by walking according to our own spirit. This is because they are one, and therefore to walk in one is to walk in the other. We must realise that our spirit is a new creation in Christ, and we must decide to live our lives as a spirit, instead of following what our flesh wants. This is why Paul said:

> [24] And those *who are* Christ's have crucified the flesh with its passions and desires.
> (Galatians 5:24)

Paul uses the metaphor of crucifixion to refer to the believer's attitude towards his flesh. The believer is to live as though his flesh was dead. The reason for this is because the flesh is where the sinful nature lives. That's why Paul said:

> [22] For I delight in the law of God according to the inward man. [23] But I see another law in my members, warring

> against the law of my mind, and bringing me into captivity to the law of sin which is in my members.
> (Romans 7:22-23)

Paul stated that the law of sin (i.e. the sinful nature) was in his "members". In other words, it was in the various parts of his body. That's why he also said:

> For I know that in me (that is, in my flesh) nothing good dwells
> (Romans 7:18)

Evidently, our bodies are born with this sinful nature, having inherited it from Adam. We know that this is the case from the simple observation that you do not need to teach a baby to do bad things (such as lying etc.); you need to teach the child to do good. But thanks be to God, when Jesus comes again, our bodies will be saved, and we will receive a new body that is just like Jesus' body (Philippians 3:21).

In the mean time, we must refuse to live according to the flesh, and instead live according to our spirit. This philosophy is echoed in Romans 8:10, where Paul wrote the following:

> [10] And if Christ *is* in you, the body *is* dead because of sin, but the Spirit *is* life because of righteousness.
> (Romans 8:10)

As far as the Christian is concerned, their body is dead because of sin. That is, because the sin nature dwells in the body, the body must now be considered to be dead. Failure to consider it "dead" will mean that the sin nature will have power over the believer. However, Paul doesn't stop there. He goes on to say, "but the Spirit is life because of righteousness". In other words, instead of living according the body, we now live according to the Spirit, and it is when we follow the Spirit that we are able to live in righteousness.

If we want the glory of who we are in Christ to shine in our lives, then we need to live according to the Holy Spirit; and we do that by following our spirit. When we live according to our new spiritual nature in Christ, we are walking in the Holy Spirit, as our spirit and the Holy Spirit have become one.

The problem for many believers is that they are so focused on the physical realm, that they are not sensitive to the reality of their new spiritual nature in Christ. Consequently, they are not able to live according to their spirit, because they are too busy looking after the flesh and following their soulish nature, instead of letting their souls be transformed by the renewing of their minds. Whilst we are not to constantly neglect the legitimate needs of our bodies and souls, when we allow either the body or soul to dominate us, we become what the Bible calls "carnal" and "sensual". The word "carnal" translates the Greek word *sarkikos* which comes from the Greek word for "flesh" (*sarx*) (1 Corinthians 3:3; Romans 8:1). The word "sensual" (James 3:15) translates the Greek word *psuchikos*, which is from the word *psuchē,* which means "soul". Instead of being carnal and sensual, we are to be *spiritual* people (1 Corinthians 3:1). This means that we are to be led by our spirit, and not by our soul or body.

The key to being led by our spirit is to daily make that decision to follow our spirit instead of our flesh, and then to take active steps to increase our sensitivity to our spirit. When we are more sensitive to our spirit, than we are to our flesh and soul, our spirit will dominate our lives, and we will be radiating the glory that dwells within us.

We will now briefly explore five ways that we can develop sensitivity to our spirit:

1. Feed on God's Word

Jesus said:

> The words that I speak to you are spirit, and *they* are life. (John 6:63)

The nature of God's word is "spirit". You are what you eat, and so when you feed on God's spiritual food, you will become stronger in spiritual things. You will be empowered to walk according to your new spiritual nature. Perhaps a reason that many believers are more sensitive to the physical realm, than they are to the spiritual realm, is because they spend more time eating physical food than they do eating spiritual food. Always remember, you are what eat! It is therefore important that we make time to feed ourselves with God's word on a daily basis.[2]

---

[2] For help with understanding the Bible, please see Dr. Pattico's book *Making Sense of the Bible* available from WWW.STUARTPATTICO.COM

2. Think Spiritual Thoughts

Paul wrote:

> ⁵ For those who live according to the flesh set their minds on the things of the flesh, but those *who live* according to the Spirit, the things of the Spirit. ⁶ For to be carnally minded *is* death, but to be spiritually minded *is* life and peace.
> (Romans 8:5-6)

This passage reveals a simple key to walking successfully in the Spirit. If we think about fleshly things, we will end up living according to the flesh. But if we think about spiritual things, we will live according to the Spirit. As we focus our thoughts on spiritual things, we will be more sensitive to our spirit. Focusing on carnal things will mean that we are more sensitive to our fleshly nature. Not only are we what we eat; to a large extent, we are also what we think!

What type of thoughts constitute spiritual thoughts? Paul tells us in Philippians 4:8:

> Finally, brethren, whatever things are true, whatever things *are* noble, whatever things *are* just, whatever things *are* pure, whatever things *are* lovely, whatever things *are* of good report, if *there is* any virtue and if *there is* anything praiseworthy—meditate on these things.
> (Philippians 4:8)

Let us ensure that such things are our focus.

3. Fellowship with God

In John 4:24, Jesus states that "God is Spirit". The nature of God is spirit. Therefore, when we fellowship with Him, we are acquainting ourselves with our true nature, which is "spirit". As we are made in God's image, and God is "Spirit", we must therefore be "spirit" too, as the image of God is a spiritual image. When we fellowship with Him, we become aware of the reality of "Spirit" and encounter the One from whom our spiritual image is derived.

It is important that we fellowship with God throughout the day. After all, He has promised us: "I will never leave you nor forsake you" (Hebrews 13:5). This indicates that God is with us at all points of the day. How would you like it if you were to spend the day with someone, and they didn't speak to you for the whole day? Well, God is with us always, and it is important that we commune with Him throughout the day.

In addition to communing with God during the day, it is also important that we take out special time to spend with Him, to adore Him, to pray, and to hear His voice. Jesus said,

> But you, when you pray, go into your room, and when you have shut your door, pray to your Father who *is* in the secret *place;* and your Father who sees in secret will reward you openly.
> (Matthew 6:6)

In so doing, our affection towards, and experience of God is taken to new heights, as we learn what it is to be lost in His presence.

Paul indicates that the marriage relationship of a man and woman points to the relationship to Christ with His church:

> [31] "For this reason a man shall leave his father and mother and be joined to his wife, and the two shall become one flesh." [32] This is a great mystery, but I speak concerning Christ and the church.
> (Ephesians 5:31-32)

This indicates that the Lord wants to have an intimate relationship with His people. Within marriage, Paul explains to us how that the husband and wife are not to withhold themselves from each other:

> Let the husband render to his wife the affection due her, and likewise also the wife to her husband. The wife does not have authority over her own body, but the husband *does*. And likewise the husband does not have authority over his own body, but the wife *does*.
> (1 Corinthians 7:3-4)

Even so, in the divine marriage of Christ and His church, we are not to withhold our spirit from Jesus. And, if I may say so, Jesus is not to withhold His Spirit from us (for He will not violate His own principle!) This is why we do not need to struggle to get into God's presence. We do not need to struggle in order to experience His Spirit. He simply invites all who are thirsty to come!

4. Pray in Other Tongues

If we wish to become sensitive to our spirit, then it is very important that we practice the privilege of praying in other tongues. Praying in tongues is a way that our spirit prays to God. Paul made this clear in the following verse:

> [14] For if I pray in a tongue, **my spirit prays**, but my understanding is unfruitful.
> (1 Corinthians 14:14)

When we pray in tongues, it is not our mind praying. That is why Paul says, "my understanding is unfruitful". Your mind, will, and emotions constitute your soul. Therefore, when you pray in tongues, it is not your soul praying. Instead, Paul said, "my spirit prays". When you pray in tongues, it is your born-again spirit that is doing the praying. The more time you spend praying in tongues, is the more you develop sensitivity to your spirit, as it is your spirit that is doing the praying. You will begin to sense what your spirit feels like. You will experience a flow in your spirit as you are praying in tongues, and so you will grow in sensitivity to your spiritual person.

The ability to pray to God in tongues is available to all believers. This ability is to be distinguished from the gift of giving a message in tongues to the church (which can then be interpreted). That is a different gift altogether, and not everyone will be used in that gift (as Paul makes clear in 1 Corinthians 12:30). The ability to pray to God in tongues is quite different. It can be used in private, in your own personal times of prayer with God. The result of its use is that it edifies the person praying in tongues:

> [4] He who speaks in a tongue edifies himself...
> (1 Corinthians 14:4)

The Greek word translated "edifies" means to build a house. When you pray in tongues, you are building yourself stronger and more powerful in God. No wonder the apostle Paul was such a powerful man of God, he prayed in tongues more than all the Corinthians put together!

> I thank my God I speak with tongues more than you all
> (1 Corinthians 14:18)

Clearly Paul spent a lot of time praying in tongues. If we wish to release the glory that is inside us, we should spend time doing the same. If you are new to the concept of praying in tongues, you may wish to start by spending 5 minutes a day praying in tongues. You can then increase this to 10 minutes, then 15 minutes, then 30 minutes etc.

If you do not have the ability to pray in tongues, and would like to receive this gift, please follow the instructions in the Appendix. Also, more detailed information about the power of praying in tongues is available in my book *Praying with Power*.

5. Honour the Way of Love

We have seen that we can follow the Holy Spirit by following our own spirit, as they have become one. When we live according to our spirit, we will fulfil the righteous requirement of God's law. As Paul said:

> [4] that the righteous requirement of the law might be fulfilled in us who do not walk according to the flesh but according to the Spirit.
> (Romans 8:4)

Paul also told us that the entire law is fulfilled by the following single commandment:

> [4] For all the law is fulfilled in one word, *even* in this: "You shall love your neighbor as yourself."
> (Galatians 5:14)

Therefore, when we live according to our spirit, we will be walking in love, as fulfilling the righteousness of the law is the result of walking according to the Spirit. We have seen that the glory of God is in our spirit. However, John informs us that "God is love" (1 John 4:8). Therefore, to claim to be walking according to the Spirit, and not walk in love is a contradiction. Our spirit has been recreated according to the likeness of God. Regarding this, Paul states:

> ...put on the new man which was created according to God, in true righteousness and holiness.
> (Ephesians 4:24)

The new man has been created "according to God". As "God is love", our spirit is therefore filled with His love. This means that our spirit *wants* to love people. It is impossible to walk according to your spirit and not walk in love, because the love of God is in your spirit.

When we are walking in love we will not gossip or say bad things about each other. About this, James wrote:

> [11] Do not speak evil of one another, brethren. He who speaks evil of a brother and judges his brother, speaks evil of the law and judges the law. But if you judge the law, you are not a doer of the law but a judge.
> (James 4:11)

We are plainly told not to "speak evil of one another". I wonder how different our churches would be if we adhered to this simple commandment. To speak "evil" simply means to say things that are negative about others.

Furthermore, when we walk in love, we will seek each other's well being. Paul wrote that "love does no harm to a neighbor" (Romans 13:10). He also wrote that "love edifies"(1 Corinthians 8:1). In other words, love builds up others, it doesn't tear them down; it only seeks their good.

The following well-known passage describes what love is:

> [4] Love is patient, love is kind. It does not envy, it does not boast, it is not proud. [5] It does not dishonor others, it is not self-seeking, it is not easily angered, it keeps no record of wrongs. [6] Love does not delight in evil but rejoices with the truth. [7] It always protects, always trusts, always hopes, always perseveres. [8] Love never fails...
> (1 Corinthians 13:4-8 NIV)

A simple way to test if our actions and thoughts are consistent with the way of love is to compare them with the description in that passage. Paul tells us both what love is, and also what love is not. It is patient, kind, protective, trusting, hopeful, persevering, and it rejoices in the truth. But, love is not envious, boastful, proud, dishonouring, self-seeking, or easily angered, nor does it delight in evil. Let us endeavour always to walk in the way of love.

Reflective Questions:

Are you happy with the amount of time you spend in God's Word?

Think about how you could increase the amount of time you are spending in God's Word. Begin to implement your thoughts.

Do you consciously fellowship with God throughout the day?

Throughout the day, what kind of things do you think about? Would you describe them as fleshly or spiritual thoughts?

Do you take out special time to spend with God in your daily routine?

What place does praying in tongues have in your prayer life?

How is your love walk? Is there anyone you are not walking in love towards?

Conclusion

Let me share with you a quick testimony which I hope will encourage you to see the glory that abides within you. I was at a funeral and I came across a lady who was in a wheelchair. She said to me that she had to share a testimony with me, and went on to say that since I touched her she has been able to walk more, she's now been able to take steps and walk more. Her nerves are getting stronger and stronger, and she said she had to share this testimony with me. As she was sharing, to be honest, I didn't remember ever praying with her. I enquired of her and she explained that I shook her hand. She had come to a conference, and I was speaking there. I greeted her as I would anyone else. She said that when I shook her hand, she felt the power of God go into her body. And ever since that time, she's been able take steps and her nerves are getting stronger. I didn't even pray for her, in fact, I didn't even feel power leave me! It was simply the fact that I, like you, am a carrier of God's glory!

Paul's prayer was that they would know "what are the riches of the glory of His inheritance in the saints". Do you have any idea what you are carrying? I am not talking about something you will one day carry if you fast enough, or if you pray enough. I am talking about the glory that is in your spirit right now. God wants to give you a spirit of revelation so that your eyes would be enlightened so that you may realise what is really in you, because this world needs what you are carrying. The world needs what is inside of you! You are carrying God's glory!

Conclusion

Appendix – Receiving the Gift of Praying in Tongues

If you have not yet been activated in your prayer language, here are some steps that you can follow in order to freely receive this wonderful gift:

1. Get into the presence of God

You can enter God's presence by praising Him:

> Enter into His gates with thanksgiving,
> *And* into His courts with praise.
> Be thankful to Him, *and* bless His name.
> (Psalm 100:4)

As you enter into His presence with praise, you are ready for the next step.

2. Ask God to fill you with His Spirit and to give you your prayer language

Jesus said:

> Until now you have asked nothing in My name. Ask, and you will receive, that your joy may be full.
> (John 16:24)

If you've already been filled with the Holy Spirit, that's fine, just ask God to fill you anyway. The Bible teaches that we are to be continuously filled with the Spirit (Ephesians 5:18). If you haven't yet been filled with the Holy Spirit, get ready, because you are about to be!

So, simply ask God to fill you with His Spirit and to give you your prayer language. And then move on to the next step.

3. Believe that you have received

Jesus said:

> ... whatever things you ask **when you pray, believe that you receive *them*,** and you will have *them*.
> (Mark 11:24)

This is very important. Once you have asked God to fill you with His Spirit, you must believe that He has done so; you must accept and believe that it is done. Verbalise your faith by saying, "I believe I have received, thank You Lord for filling me with Your Spirit and for giving me the gift of praying in other tongues". Then you can move on to the next step:

4. Stop speaking in English

You are about to speak in other tongues, but you can't speak in two languages at the same time! Therefore, stop speaking in your native language, and get ready to speak in other tongues. It is very important that you do not speak another word in your native language.

5. Begin to speak in other tongues

The Holy Spirit will not force you to speak in tongues. Notice that in Acts 2:4, the Bible doesn't say that the Holy Spirit spoke in tongues, it says that "they" (i.e. those who were filled) spoke in tongues:

> And **they**... began to speak with other tongues, as the Spirit gave them utterance.
> (Acts 2:4)

When Jesus came walking on water to the disciples, He didn't force Peter to get out of the boat and start walking on the water.

> [26] And when the disciples saw Him walking on the sea, they were troubled, saying, "It is a ghost!" And they cried out for fear.
> [27] But immediately Jesus spoke to them, saying, "Be of good cheer! It is I; do not be afraid."
> [28] And Peter answered Him and said, "Lord, if it is You, command me to come to You on the water."
> [29] So He said, "Come." And when Peter had come down out of the boat, he walked on the water to go to Jesus.
> (Matthew 14:26-29)

Peter had to make a decision to get out of the boat, and then to walk on water. Peter had to leave what he knew (the boat) and step out into the unknown (the water). Peter didn't know He could walk on water until He tried, and you won't know you can speak in tongues until you try. So, you need to stop speaking in English (get out of the boat, leave the known) and start speaking the syllables that flow forth from your spirit (walk on water, you don't know you can until you put your foot on the water and try!).

You won't necessarily hear new words in your mind. You just need to start speaking in faith the syllables that will flow forth from your spirit, and God will form them into your new prayer language. Just trust Him, He will do it!

I encourage you to take the time right now to follow those five steps, and to allow God to give you this blessing.

Contact Dr. Stuart & Minister Andrea Pattico

To invite Dr. Stuart Pattico to speak at your church or event, please visit WWW.STUARTPATTICO.COM where you can contact him. His wife, Minister Andrea Pattico is also available to speak and lead worship at worship events. They can both be contacted via the website.

Other Books by Dr. Stuart Pattico

End Times: Are You Prepared?

Hearing God's Voice

Discover and Fulfil Your Purpose

The Anointing

Interpret Your Dreams

Making Sense of the Bible

Moving in the Prophetic

Praying with Power

These resources are available from:

WWW.STUARTPATTICO.COM

Join Our Mailing List

Our website, WWW.STUARTPATTICO.COM contains free videos that you can watch, and articles that you can read. On this site, you can also join the free mailing list by submitting your email address. You will then receive regular ministry updates, and notifications when new items are added to this site.

Become a Ministry Partner

If you would like to help financially support Dr. Pattico's full-time ministry, you can do so by either making a one-off donation, or by making automatic monthly payments. Please visit the donations section of our website for more information:

WWW.STUARTPATTICO.COM

Publish Your Book With Us!

Would you like us to publish your book? Sunesis Ministries enables Christian authors to publish their God-given books.

For more information about our low-cost, professional publishing package, please contact us via our website:

WWW.STUARTPATTICO.COM